TO CATCH THE RAINBOW

BOOK ONE

"THE CYPRIOT STORY"

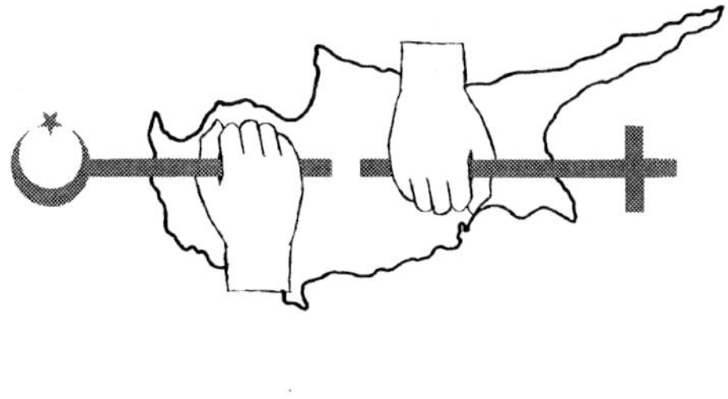

by

GOKALP KAMIL

First published May 1997

First edition

ISBN 975-94744-0-9

Cover design by Gökalp Kamil

Computer Graphics by Semray Sucuoğlu

Printed by Dörtrenk Matbaacılık Ltd. - Lefkoşa

Gökalp at the age of 15.

On a warm and sunny day in May the boy of sixteen had his suitcase packed and ready for a journey that would perhaps never bring him back to the land of his birth, or to his family and friends. His thoughts were of the excitement of flying, of the journey ahead and of seeing the places he had read about in his books at school or been told of by his teachers; of meeting the people of the world who controlled his world and his life.

He was awakened that morning by the servant of his host and mentor, Sir Eric Hallinan, the chief justice of Cyprus, who had taken the responsibility for the young boy only four days before his flight from the Island. But unknown to the boy, Sir Eric had been his protector before that and had in fact first taken an interest in him a few months earlier, in March, when dossiers of a terrorist act had been brought to his attention.

When he came downstairs, the boy entered the breakfast room where he found Sir Eric already seated and halfway through his breakfast. He wished his protector good morning and sat down at the table where his place was laid. Their conversation that morning was the last they would ever have, but Sir Eric, until his tragic death just over a year later, would follow the boy's life from afar.

"Sir, I wish to thank you for all you have done for me".

Sir Eric did not reply to this but carried on a

conversation and talked of the pleasantness of the morning. When breakfast was finally over Sir Eric said:

"You are going to a different world. The real world. It is up to you what you make of it. I am going to my office now and will send the car back to take you to the airport. Goodbye to you and good luck".

That was the last time this boy saw his protector of the last few months for they were fated never to meet again. But the memory of the old man lived on with him and many times in later life he thought fondly of him. Had it not been for this kind old man, the boy would have died at the hands of the terrorists.

* * * * *

The Island of Love. The beautiful land of Cyprus. The Island of Aphrodite Goddess of Love, was still, in 1955, with its language of Homeric prose and its way of life, little changed since ancient times; suddenly it became the "Island of Perdition".

* * * * *

In the early hours of the morning of 1st April 1955, the quietness of the city of Nicosia was shattered by the sound of exploding bombs. The boy was staying there with his cousin for a few days, and like every other inhabitant of the city he was woken up by the explosions. Later that morning he took to the streets with the enthusiasm and curiosity of the young to find out their cause.

He did not have to go far to find out. The conversation on the streets, in front of every shop, in the cafes, and among the people walking by was loud and excited enough for him to hear what had taken place without having to ask. He decided to go and see for himself where the explosions had taken place, with no thought other than the inquisitiveness of the young. The events of the night as far as he was concerned had nothing to do with him. All that interested him was the unexpected diversion from the day's normal run, for this provided him with an excuse to explore those parts of the city unknown to him until now. Little did he know that the events of that night would in less than a year have him caught up in their web, and that the echoes of the explosions of that night were but the sounds announcing his future.

* * * * *

And it was just over a year later to that fateful day, again in Nicosia, when, in the twilight, unexpectedly, he was picked up by the Police under the ancient walls of the city by the Kyrenia Gate and was brought to the residence of the Chief Justice in a Land Rover with an armed escort. He had no idea why or for what purpose.

That morning he had gone with his English teacher, Mr Rofe, to Larnaca. Normally he would have spent the day, after school, at his friend's house on the outskirts of the city as he had done since his arrival in Nicosia. But the weather was pleasantly warm and he had been glad to accept his teacher's invitation. They left quite early and spent the whole day seeing places of interest, walking in the town and visiting the Holy Shrine of Ummu Haram Rumeyissa bint-i Milhan, near the salt lake. Ummu Haram Rumeyissa bint-i Milhan means Holy Mother Lady of the Romans doughter of the Saltseller if not the Milkseller but more likely in the local vernacular of the Western Semitic dialect bint-i Milhan, the doughter of the King, was the maternal aunt of the Prophet Mohammed who according to tradition had wet-nursed the infant Prophet Mohammed; a tradition which is, indeed, much older then Islam and Christianity that has carried to our day in unbroken continuity of a traditional value since the Ancient of Days long before Prophet Jeremiah wrote: "For pass over the isles of Chittim, and see; and send unto Kedar, and consider diligently, and see if there be such a thing. Hath a nation changed their gods, which are yet no gods?" (Chapter 2 verses 10, 11. Chittim is the Biblical name for Cyprus, Kedar is Mecca as well as the names of the kings of Mecca before and at the time Jeremiah wrote his book, which was long before the bishops of Rome's, the popes, concept of Christianity came into being in the eleventh century AD for political purposes to oppose the religion of the Romans established by Constantine the Great; and long before the Bible was translated into Latin in the fourth century AD, supposedly by Jerome on the order of Damasus, the bishop of Rome; and, probably, long before the Greeks from Euboea took the alphabet from the Phoenicians at a place called Al Mina.) Gokalp had been to the shrine before with his mother and grandmother and once on an outing with his school from Paphos. It was there at the tekke of Hala Sultan that he learned from his grandmother the fate of the aunt of the Prophet Mohammed who had Left Mecca to come to Cyprus. The Holy Lady fell off her horse and died while visiting the tomb of holy personage of the line of prophets, and was buried there.

They caught the last bus back to Nicosia. It had been a perfect day. He was very pleased to have had this opportunity to talk English with his teacher. Both because he much enjoyed it and because he looked upon it as a fine chance to learn. The bus was stopped by the Police in the suburbs of the city. They would not allow it to pass, saying that there had been an incident and that part of the city was under curfew.

His teacher left the bus to speak to the police officer controlling the barricade. He returned to the bus and told the boy that he had obtained permission to walk into town with him. They left the bus and walked away leaving behind the other passengers to object and argue their plight to the policemen at the barricade.

By the time they arrived at the Kyrenia Gate it was getting dark and people were gathering for their evening walk and enjoyment under the Walls of the Turkish Quarter of this ancient city, where the curfew did not apply.

After taking leave of his teacher, he decided to look for his friends and wandered off to where they were likely to be found.

When he found them, not far away underneath one of the eucalyptus trees, he was greeted with excitement and asked where had he been. The police were looking for him, they told him, and had instructed them to keep him where he was if he turned up. Two of his friends went running a few hundred yards to where the city police headquarters were situated in Kyrenia street.

Within a short while an officer with an armed escort had arrived in a Land Rover and the boy was taken to the residence of the Chief Justice.

On the way he tried to find out what was going on and why he was being taken to the Chief Justice. But the police officer in charge would only say that his instructions were to take him there safe and sound, and that they had been looking for him since the afternoon and that the reason for the curfew was evident.

Yet the boy could not understand what was happening. The Land Rover stopped before a huge gate. All he could see were the guards at the entrance and opposite was an even larger gate with the Royal Coat of Arms above it, carved on a plaque let into the stone wall.

The gate opened and the Land Rover slowly moved

through and along the driveway to the front of the house. There standing at the top of the steps, was a tall, white haired, lean man.

The Land Rover came to a halt. The officer got out and told the boy to follow him, then stood at the bottom of the steps and saluted. Sir Eric thanked the officer and, turning to the boy, he said:

"So you are found. Come with me."

The boy followed him into the house, to a large living room. There another surprise was in waiting for him. Mr Rofe, his English teacher with whom he had gone to Larnaca, was standing by the door to the terrace with a broad smile on his face. Sir Eric formally introduced himself saying:

"I am Sir Eric Hallinan. Chief Justice of Cyprus. You are to stay with me for a few days until a safe place can be found for you. Meanwhile you will be quite safe here." A servant appeared at the door as if summoned by unheard command and was asked to bring lemonade and some sandwiches for the boy.

Telling him to sit down, Sir Eric said:

"You are a very lucky boy to be alive."

Before the sandwiches and the lemonade were served Sir Eric and Mr Rofe spoke briefly together on the terrace. When they came back into the room his teacher told the boy:

"The EOKA terrorists have discovered your whereabouts. They called there this afternoon. Lucky you were with me at Larnaca. They would have killed you there and then. You are safe now and here."

Next morning the boy was taken by Sir Eric's driver to collect his belongings from his school dormitory, where he had been staying ever since the day he was delivered to his father's care at Kyrenia Gate police station and that is when he learned from his friends what had happened the previous afternoon. Three of them had gathered at the friend's house, on the outskirts of town, to await his arrival. They did not know he had gone to Larnaca.

They saw a car stop in front of the house. Three men got out and walked straight in. As they came through the front door they pulled out guns and forced the boys against the wall of the room.

One of the men then said "Which of you is Gokalp?" At which his friends in shock and fear shook their heads and replied that none of them was he. The terrorist asking the questions then took Shevket, one of his friends, by the throat and pressed him hard against the wall. He pointed the gun between his eyes and said that he would shoot him because he did not believe him and added that in fact he thought that he was Gokalp. They were all very frightened.

The EOKA terrorist then turned to one of his gunmen and told him to bring someone from the car. A few moments later a girl appeared at the door with this man. The terrorist with his hand at the throat of Shevket asked her:

"Is this him?"
The girl shook her head and whispered "No."

Then the terrorist pointed at the two other boys and asked again:

"Is he one of those?"

Again the girl shook her head. The man released his grip on the throat of Shevket and with a gesture of his head ordered the girl and the third man to get out. Picking his words carefully and speaking slowly and with menace, the EOKA terrorist moved from boy to boy looking each one in the eye and said:

"You are not to move out of this room or go anywhere for the next half hour. Tell Gokalp we will get him."

Then, with deliberate steps, he walked out of the front door followed by the second terrorist, to the car.

The three boys stood there as if frozen for what seemed to them like almost half an hour. Then they started to argue about what to do. They finally decided to get out of the house and run to the police together, rather than one by one. It had actually only taken eleven minutes from the moment the terrorist walked up to the front door until the boys reached the police.

* * * * *

Gokalp's few days stay with Sir Eric passed pleasantly. They took a drive in the afternoon to Bogaz, in Sir Eric's black Ford Consul car with Sir Eric at the driving wheel and his driver body guard, a Greek Cypriot man, in the front passenger seat, seeing along the way the villagers returning to their village on donkeys, having spent the day selling or buying essentials at the market. Then in the evening they drank lemonade and talked on the patio and after dinner they talked again. But this time Sir Eric acted as a teacher, recording the boy's voice on the newly available and expensive Grundig tape recorder and playing it back, so that his mistakes could be pointed out. Hearing his voice for the very first time was not only amusing but the deepness of its tone was a revelation to him.

Unknown to him while he thus passed his time, conferences were taking place in Nicosia and in London, coded telexes were being sent to and fro and decisions were being taken. The most important of these concerned his immediate safety, for he could not stay there indefinitely with Sir Eric. So it was decided to send him immediately to his uncle in Istanbul, until permanent arrangements could be made for his future and education.

Why was he wanted by the terrorists? Why did they want to kill him? What had he done? This was not the first time they had tried to kill him. This boy, who grew up with the children of Greek Cypriots and had many friends among them, who spoke their language fluently and could write it just as well: whose childhood and formative years were influenced by Cypriot Greeks who lived and worked in the same street: for the town of Paphos where he was born and grew up, consisted of no more than a couple of thousand inhabitants in all. Greeks, Turks, Armenian, Maronites, all of whom knew each other and had lived together for centuries under the Imperial Ottoman context of world order. Even the town itself had remained unchanged for hundreds of years.

On his last evening in bed under the protection of Sir Eric and knowing that next day would be the start of a new life, he reflected back to his childhood in Paphos and to the events that took him there.

★ ★ ★ ★ ★

His recollection of his early childhood consisted mostly of the times spent with his mother, grandmothers, and grandfathers. All he could remember of his father was his return from Egypt after the end of the war in 1946. He was six years old by then.

He remembered his father's return to Paphos bringing the sergeant-major, Regimental Sergeant Major McMahon as a guest to their house. His father held the rank of sergeant. It was the panayir time when for one week the town and the surrounding villages would come together to enjoy themselves. This was the fair celebrating the end of silk yarn production, the origins of which go back at least for centuries if not a millennium.

For the townspeople the excitement in anticipation of the fair would start with the dismantling of the looms and the cauldrons in which the silk cocoons were boiled, and, levelling of the stone and earth fireplaces containing the cauldrons; and on the arrival of the first trader to the fairground. This always attracted a large crowd from the neighbourhood. Children would gather around and watch the pitching of a tent and unloading of merchandise. One by one merchants from all over the Island would come in horse drawn carts or on mules and even with caravans of camels. In those days mechanised transport was rare.

They would pitch their tents in the field at the top of the street where the cauldrons and the looms had stood. Some would set up stalls in front of the houses and inside empty silk or carob stores. The fair would start at dusk and continue into the early hours; there was no electricity then, the lighting was done by pressurised paraffin lamps.

Everything there was for sale from sweets made from boiled sugar cast in metal moulds in the shape of animals which looked like delicate glass ornaments, to gold bracelets, earrings and necklaces and lokmas, koftes, kebabs and lamb cooked in large urns made into ovens.

Games of chance were played, strong men performed their acts of strength and gypsies told fortunes; and in a dark and empty store at the edge of the fair they showed the silent movie "Journey to the Moon" by the Loumière Brothers.

Here for one week people paraded up and down, shopping, eating roast lamb cooked in large urns, crushed wheat koftes filled with fried onions or hot crunchy lokmas dipped in honey syrup or sprinkled with sugar and rose water. Playing games of chance, having their fortunes told. Here a rich headman of a village dressed in his boots, baggy kilt, cummerbund wound around the waist and a richly embroidered waistcoat over a collarless silk shirt, woven locally on a hand loom, and a scarf wound over the head, would walk, his head proudly held high, sporting on his upper lip the upturned Kaiserian moustache, behind his drably dressed wife in grey or black long sleeved and long skirted coat like dress, her hair and head tightly covered in a dark head scarf. Turkish women covered from head to toe in black silk charshaphe walked in front of their husbands, only their eyes visible to the outside world. Some hid the eyes behind a tulle in the unchanged biblical fashion of a high born lady. The high born ladies' husbands were attired in sartorial three piece suits that marked their stations in life. Here also walked their daughters, in their smart western fashionable clothes and hair styles with their husbands and young children, boys dressed in sailor's outfits, girls as Shirley Temples. Their husbands usually the most respected men in town, either doctors or lawyers, walked with self assured professional pride in their double breasted striped suits. Here also walked people who wore the same clothes every day of the year summer or winter. And in contrast to all this soldiers on leave in their khaki shirts and shorts attracted more attention. They were soldiers and also sons, husbands and fathers who came back from the war.

At the fair rich farmers and merchants would buy jewellry for their wives, peasants would buy them as a dowry for their daughters. They would also buy all sorts of cloth and pottery, for in those days most of the cooking utensils and water jugs were made of clay: glass, leather, dried milk produce, pulse, in fact every thing that was essential or a luxury to their lives was sold in an enlivened atmosphere of bargaining and pleasure. In the middle of this sea of wavering people stood, like the bow of a cruise liner, on the narrow angle of the upturned Y of the merging roads, Marahefti's store. Marahefti lived above the store. The large terrace above looked like the deck of a liner riding the wave of people going to and fro. This completed the surreal painting in the memory of the boy, in the year his father returned from the war.

This was the biggest event of the year for the town. Everybody saw every one else and exchanged gossip. New friendships were formed and old ones renewed. Children wanted this never to end. Young men and girls eyed each other or exchanged words or glances that later developed into passion consummated behind a tree or a bush in the darkness of the night only a few yards from this hive of

Gökalp's father İbrahim Derviş Kamil.

Halide Hüseyin the expectant mother and İbrahim Derviş Kamil on their wedding day.

Gökalp with paternal grandfather Derviş and grandmother Saffet.

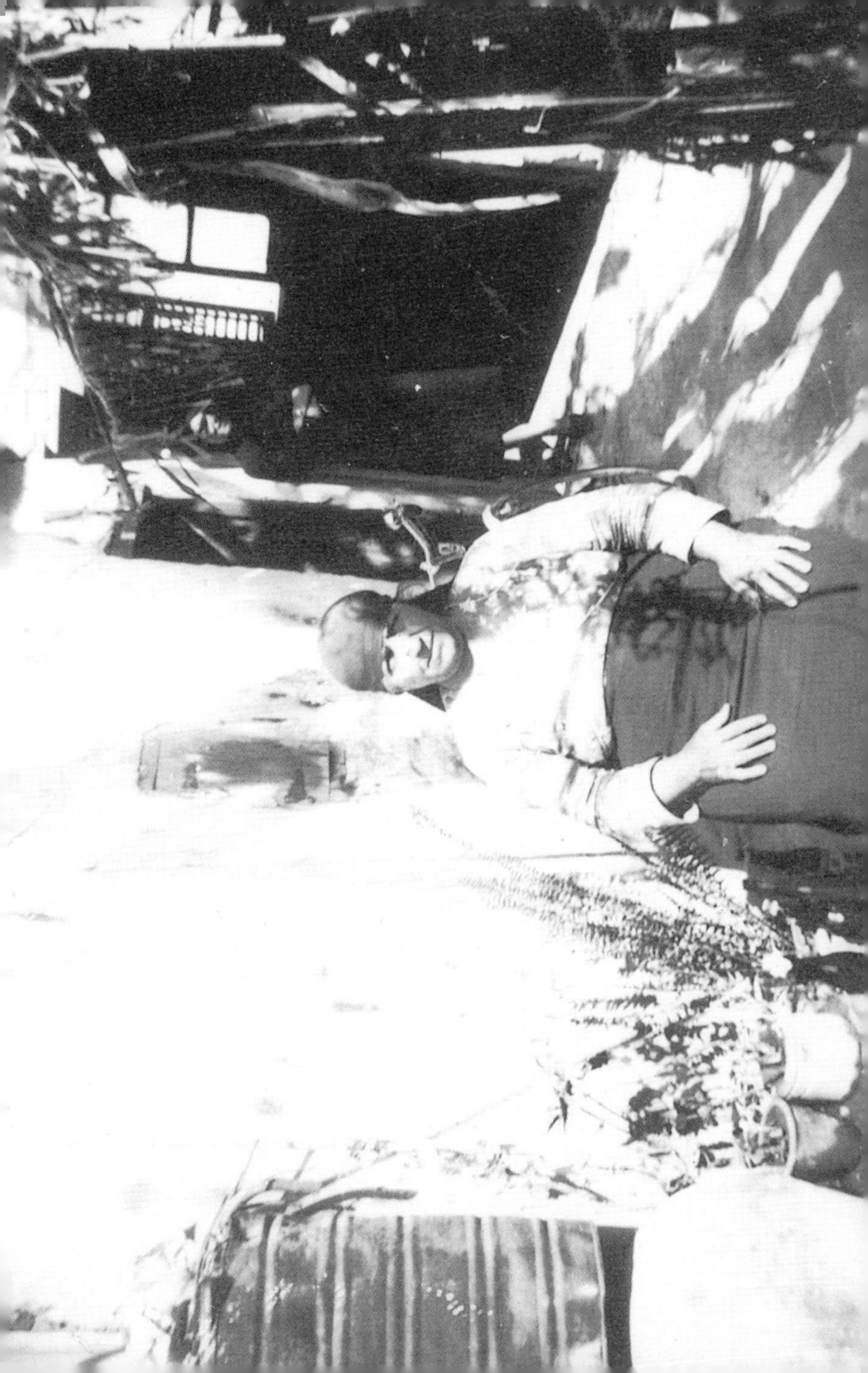

Grandmother Ulfet. Picture taken in the 1950's.

Grandmother Ulfet with uncle Kemal as a child. Picture taken in 1919.

Gökalp's mother as a young girl with her brother Kemal, seated, and Adnan.

A landau (carrutsa) and it's occupants, after visiting the holy shrine of Hala Sultan near the salt lake, poseing with two other visitor on their donkey's. Picture taken 1878.

activity. Some were caught, usually by someone in a hurry to relieve himself. For those unfortunates and their families it meant scandal and an unplanned wedding or a divorce at the earliest possible time.

In his memory this was the best year of the fair. Also it was the only time he had the approval and the attention of his father. Holding onto his hand on one side and that of the R.S.M. on the other, walking between them in their uniforms, the boy felt the world was his.

The fair started on the Saturday and the R.S.M. McMahon left on the Monday. The fair ended the following Sunday and his father left a few days afterwards.

* * * * *

His father had joined the British Army after Gokalp was born in 1940 because it was a decently paid profession, as did most young men from the town. There was no other employment for them available. It did not matter that they were going to war. He rose to the rank of Sergeant and spent the last year of the war in Alexandria. Then served a further three years in Palestine. On his demobilisation in 1949 he returned to Cyprus and enrolled in the Police force where, after a short period of training and service, he was given his old army rank of Sergeant.

His mother had married his father when she was thirteen and he was twenty five. By the time he was demobilised they already had three children and another was on the way; so it went on and after several abortions or self induced miscarriages, they finally ended up with eleven children altogether.

The house where they lived was one up, two down, white washed stone built with a flat earthen roof, and had an outside stairway and a balcony made of wood. Here he spent his childhood, with his mother and his maternal grandmother and grandfather. As the family grew, more rooms were added one by one. They had a large garden full of almond trees, figs, pomegranates, loquats, bananas and the famous gum tree of Paphos from which chewing gum was made.

The whole property was surrounded by a high stone wall. The lavatory and the bath-house were situated at the extreme end of the garden and the kitchen was next to the door from the street which opened onto a courtyard in front of the house. In the summer, most of the cooking was done outside in the open on a stone fireplace burning wood. In the winter, it was done inside on a paraffin burner that replaced wood. Here he watched his grandmother cooking.

In the evenings in winter they would sit in the downstairs room, around the circular copper hearth filled with glowing charcoals, warming themselves, roasting chestnuts in the ashes and listening to stories told by his grandmother. Her stories were dramatised, more so on stormy nights, by the flickering light of the oil lamp that made the shadows move to the howling of the wind outside blown into the room through the gaps in the wooden shutters. Lightning and crack of thunder that strafed through the room when the storm raged overhead; or the roaring of the high seas pounding the rocks, a mile away, at the tombs of ancient kings of Paphos were the background effects to her stories of monsters, dragons, giants and man with a mission in life who slew the apparitions. She painted pictures with words in his mind's eye.

In the summer they would sit outside under the stars, enthralled by more of her endless tales of princes and princesses, rich merchants and poor people, sailors and their voyages, warriors and their conquests, lovers and their misfortunes, jealous husbands and deceitful wives, poor boys becoming rich and marrying the princess, who were always wives of virtue and source of strength to their husbands.

Later when he read the Eastern classics he knew that he had lived them all before. Even the ancient Egyptian story. The story of "Rhampsinites", which had frightened him as a child, to be remembered well, was told by her without the slightest deviation from the original.

His maternal grandmother was a large and handsome woman. She had been very beautiful in her youth, her smile warm and inviting. She ruled the family by the strength of her will and charm. Everyone succumbed to her wishes in the end. Her name, Ulfet, meant sociable and friendly, which she was.

Huseyin, his maternal grandfather, for his part was a very strict person. He was by training a veterinary surgeon but after his return to Paphos, in 1924, from Istanbul where he had gone in 1918, at first ran a market garden and a cereal farm which he then transferred to his eldest son Kemal and settled himself to earn his living as a greengrocer in the municipal market, the picturesque municipal market which was built by Huseyin's maternal grandfather, Mehmed, Kabasakal Mehmed Bey. Huseyin was of slight build. It was said he took after his greatgrandfather Kucuk Mehmed. Grandfather Huseyin was very proud of his aucestors. He used to say: "We are Kabasakal, we come from a very old and noble family" and recite the names of his forefathers, amongst them Hadji Omer and Menteşezade Hadji Ismail. The only time Gokalp would see his maternal grandfather was in the evening when he returned home to have his supper and to sleep. Next morning he would be up by four o'clock to start all over again.

After supper grandfather would sit on a chair in their bedroom and grandmother would take his boots off and the bandages that bound his feet that were used as socks. Grandfather always wore tan coloured ridingboots. She then washed his feet, another tradition going back to Joseph and Asena, welcoming him with similar words uttered by Asena when Joseph appeared at the door: "come in my Lord and let me wash thy feet":

and dried them and then helped him to undress down to his woollen undershirt and long pants. Having prepared himself for bed grandfather would then sit on the edge of the high cast iron four poster bed with brass knobs and empty his pockets on the bed. This was a signal for Gokalp to jump up and help his grandfather count the takings of the day. Paper money grandfather would count again and put into a wallet. Occasionally, grandmother would join in and whenever she did she would crumple up a ten shilling note and place it in her bosom, and if ever she took a one pound note, then grandfather would make a great business of retrieving it from her. For helping out Gokalp was rewarded with a penny or a threepenny piece.

In the morning his grandmother would be the first to wake up. She would light the oil lamp. Grandfather would then get up and go out to the lavatory. When he returned she would pour water from a clay jug for grandfather to wash his face. Grandfather would then break a raw egg and swallow it and down two fingers of cognac measured out into a glass. After this he would start to dress. First he would put on the woollen cummerbund which he wound round his waist, turning round and round in a circle while grandmother held the other end; then his woollen undershirt and shirt; then his trousers and riding boots. Finally he would put on his waistcoat and jacket. He had given up wearing the traditional fez, red conical headgear; banned by the founder of the modern republic of Turkey as a sign of backwardness. Grandfather had gone along with changes brought about in the name of modernism, which were closely followed in Cyprus, and threw away the fez, but drew the line when it came to grandmother. He steadfastly and jealously stood his ground and forbade her to do away with her traditional black dress, charshaphe, made of finest silk worn only out of doors. He had walked out of the meeting, with grandmother in front, when it was suggested that those present should set an example to others by taking off their traditional dresses worn over normal dresses out of doors, there and then. Grandfather and grandmother never again attended any such gatherings.

With a smile he remembered grandmother tell the story of her first meeting grandfather. Grandfather Huseyin Remzi Mehmed had gone with his paternal aunt Havva, the daughter of Emir Huseyin, Aide de Camp to Kucuk Mehmed, after the terms and conditions for the marriage contract had been drawn up to see grandmather Ulfet Yusuf Emirzade. Grandfather wore a white linen double breasted suit with a fez for headgear, cutting a very dashing and handsome figure. It was on this very first occasion, after presenting grandmother with a golden neeklace in return which she lifted her vail for him to see her face, that grandfather took a swipe at grandmother's headgear, throwing it off. When asked by grandmother why he did that, grandfather had answered: "I was told you were bald". Grandmother was very proud of her head of hair which went down to her waist. Her beauty was enhanced by many a different way she made up her hair.

Gokalp remembered himself wearing a fez, at his own circumcision. This is the rite of spiritual purification by circumcising. At the ceremony held before the actual cutting of the foreskin he wore a fez decorated with gold ornaments. So did his younger brother and cousin Metin. On that day, he, his brother and cousin Metin were first taken from his home to the mosque on horseback. At the mosque they listened to verses of the Quran read by Hoca before the memorial service held there to honour all his ancestors who had made the trust for the upkeep of the mosque and for the poor of Medine, the city of the Prophet Mohammed. This was more of a gathering of the clan and to meet some of the elders of the community there. After the mosque they went riding through the town. On this ride they were escorted on foot as grooms by the members of the family, one to each side holding the reins. Ahead of them went the drummer and the horn blower announcing the procession.

The procession ended at home where it had began. There he was divested of his carefully and elaborately attired fez, the gold chain, and the suit and given to wear his gallabiye (pronounced djellabiye), a white long sleeved long skirted shirt dress which was worn not only in Biblical times but also by those ancient peoples of the world who introduced the rite of circumcision as a traditional value to be observed; (Gen 17:12, Exodus 12:48) and the word gallabiye into their vocabulary; more than two and a half thousand years before Christ himself was circumcised. With that he has given to the care of Salih, a cousin of his father's, who held him firm while the circumciser cut the foreskin in less time it takes to blink an eyelid.

★ ★ ★ ★ ★

Gokalp's first year of elementary schooling was, if anything, uneventful. When he resumed his elementary education the following year he was promoted to a higher class, and in his last year at elementary school he often stood in for his teachers and took classes of young boys himself.

The memories forever engraved on his vivid mind of those early days were not those of his schooling but of the time spent with craftsmen like Yorgo the cobbler; the blacksmith; Solomo the carver of altars for the churches; Ibrahim the cooper of wooden barrels and maker of coffins; Yusuf the reedweaver and basket maker; Kemal the carpenter; Spiro the photographer, cheerful and unforgettable Dino the mercer, and, of course, both his grandfathers.

The blacksmith's shop was next door to their front entrance. Here he pulled the bellows to intensify the fire to heat the metal to glowing red. Later he was shown how to work with the hammer on the anvil. Here he would watch the blacksmith Tovli make nails that Yorgo the cobbler used for the soles of the boots that the peasants wore.

Yorgo the cobbler's shop was two doors down the

street from the blacksmith's. Here he watched the cobbler make his own glue, cut the leather, stitch it, stretch it over the last, then start on the sole of the boot thus shaped and finally hammer in the studs along the rim of the sole and shape the spiky end right round in a pattern.

Across the road from the cobbler was the wood carver. Solomo would carve eagles and snakes and beautiful ornamented altars from blocks of wood. The old man - he must have been in his late seventies - would give Gokalp a piece of wood and after securing it in a vice on the bench he would show the boy how to use the chisel with the wooden mallet.

Yusef dayi, the weaver of reed matting and baskets was round the corner from the wood carver. Here he learned what is probably the most ancient craft still practised today. Yusuf dayi, he was so addressed by old men, was the second husband of Lazana hanim, the Lusignan Lady (The Lady of the Lusignans).

Kemal the carpenter was a few yards further down towards the market place. Then there was Mazlume. She was Kemal the carpenter's great aunt. She always gave Gokalp a boiled sugar whenever he passed by. Her mercer's shop was across the road from Dino's shop, just before one came to the municipal market; Then there was Spiro the photographer. His shop was on the right, on the road to the Police station. And the other end at the top of the road, past the fairground and the Turkish cemetery ever green with rosemary, on the way to the ancient settlement of Lemba, on the right after the small stone bridge, was the potter, working in clay on wheels spun by his feet, making water jugs and cooking pots, his kilns built of earth contained by stone.

Each of them showed him their particular craft. Nobody ever told him to go away because they were busy. Instead, with patience and care, they taught their craft to him.

The other childhood memories which he cherished were of the days spent on the farm with his grandfather and uncle. In autumn after the first rainfall of the year he would watch his uncle plough the softened earth with the primitive wooden plough pulled by a team of oxen. He would walk behind his uncle on the harrowed earth. The smell of earth was to him then like the smell of freshly baked bread. He loved the smell of earth just as much as the smell of freshly baked bread out of the baker's oven early in the morning. At harvest time he would spend most of the day riding on the threshing board pulled by a horse going round and round in a circle, joyriding while threshing the wheat. And when the threshing was done he would join in with the grown-ups winnowing it high to the wind that would carry away the stalks while the grain would be separated and fall to the ground. Or he would ride round, hanging on the pole of the wooden water-wheel, turned by a blindfold donkey that did not take it kindly when prodded to make it run the faster.

★ ★ ★ ★ ★

He remembered the longest journey he had ever been on until then. It was a journey from Paphos to Kyrenia, with his mother to visit his father who was on the policeman training course at the Kyrenia castle. This was after his father's demobilisation in 1949. One of the instructing officers at the castle was Ulfet's half brother Mehmed Rafik. They stayed at this uncle's house.

One day they were taken into the castle and shown the dungeons and the battlements. On top of the round bastion he looked down to the harbour of the old town and beyond. From the highest tower he saw the mountain range with its peaks and deep gorges. His father pointed to the ruins of St. Hilarion castle, once a royal residence of Lusignan kings, Queens and Princesses, perched on twin peaks above the vertical north face of the mountain like a sceptre of the glory or the folly of the past. To the east of St. Hilarion below the village of Bellapayis, among the silvery green of the olive trees he saw the remains of the abbey. In his mind he had compared the town of Kyrenia with Paphos and had found it small, yet the castle was big compared to the one at Paphos which until then, he had thought was the largest thing that had ever existed.

After their conducted tour they were given lemonade and watched the parade in the castle yard, his father among them. Later with his parents, he went bathing behind the North West tower in the pool formed by the rocks jutting out into the sea.

Wandering along the rocks, he joined some older

boys. They were jumping from the rocks into the sea and he joined them and jumped. When he surfaced he tried to stand but his feet could not find the bottom. As he sank he started to hit the water with his hands as if to hold or pull himself up. He was drowning. One of the boys just reached out and seized him. The boy who pulled him out pointed and said that a few yards to the left it was shallow and there he could play in safety. The boy was Greek. He played there for a while and then returned to his parents; but he never mentioned what had happened and they knew nothing of it.

This was his first time in the sea.

* * * * *

Upon their return to Paphos the news of the impending death of his great grandfather Yusuf, Ulfet's father, hurriedly set his grandmother and him off to Limasol. He always accompanied her on her visits to Limasol. Going back to Limasol with them was Tuncay, a niece to both Ulfet and Huseyin. For Tuncay's mother Cemaliye was Ulfet's half sister and her father Niyazi was Huseyin's younger brother. Tuncay was spending her holidays at Paphos with her aunt and uncle. On arrival at Limasol in the late afternoon, grandma hired a landau to take them to the farm, which was on the road to Nicosia at a place called Ay Thanas. The farm extended right down to the shore. It had eucalyptus trees along the front and a long drive of hanging vines leading to the courtyard of the U shaped two storied farmhouse. The small stone bridge and then the eucalyptus trees on the left and the sea to the right were the signs for the approach to the farm; after the last of the eucalyptus trees the landau would turn left and slowly drive up the long drive of hanging vines towards the farmhouse. It would come to a stop in the courtyard where they would alight. The landau then would turn and drive back to Limasol. This is how he remembered the previous visits to his great grandfather's home. On this occasion however the driver also alighted and lit the brass and black lanterns to the side of the carriage; for by the time they arrived there it was dusk. The driver then inquired after Gallica Yusuf, for this was how his great grandfather was known, and drove back.

They were met by great grandfather's third wife and grandmother's half brothers and sisters, each of whom were the same age as grandma's children and some of them even younger. There were other cousins, more correctly cousins of his mother's who were like Tuncay of the same age as Gokalp. In their excitement they soon began to make so much noise that they were reminded of the state of their great grandfather and told to be quiet. They all remained there long after the funeral. They would run to the sea in the morning and stay there until they were called back to the house.

* * * * *

Back at Paphos, by this time his memories of life at home were different from before. His father had returned from Kyrenia a policeman not a soldier, yet he saw very little of him. If he was asleep in the morning it meant that he had been on night duty; if he was not at home it meant he was on duty. The rest of the time he was out drinking and only returned home drunk late at night.

On his days off his father would drink continuously and many times he would be brought home in the afternoon or early evening by his cronies when they no longer found him amusing. This usually ended with an ugly scene and his shouting or smashing things. For Gokalp it meant a beating without cause.

As these beatings continued Gokalp tried avoiding his father or hiding in one of the rooms where he thought he would be safe from his wrath. This did not help; for he would be dragged out of his hiding place and suffer an even more severe punishment.

His grandmother and grandfather had by then moved to a different house. He would wake up in the morning to the sound of the hooves of donkeys on the cobbled street outside, wash his face, go out past the bakery with its smell of fresh bread, on past the han, the stable, where the donkeys of the villagers coming to the market with their produce were left and the smell was of a different sort, past the barber's shop, and opposite, next to the bar where his father did some of his drinking, he would buy from Rodi, the provision merchant, who came from Gisonerga, olives or hallumi cheese or halva on credit to be paid for at the end of the month when his father drew his pay.

He would carry a little book with him for the merchant to write down the purchases and the total which, instead of being balanced at the end of the month, was carried forward to the next. Sometimes payments were made but never was the balance entirely paid off. Instead the debt increased.

This first task of the morning made him feel embarrassed, as did passing the bar where his father drank. That is why when he left the shop he would always cross the road to the other side before walking back to the house.

When he got home he would slice bread, and share whatever he had purchased with his brothers and sisters. His mother would be in bed sleeping, or suffering morning sickness, whether his father was on duty or not. She would usually wake after Gokalp had left to go to school. In time he grew to resent his parents.

He hated polishing his father's regulation boots and being slapped on the face or beaten for things for which his brother should have been punished. His brother was only sixteen months younger than he was yet it seemed that he could do no wrong.

He remembered the time his father returned from a refresher course and he went with him to visit his aunt. His father had brought back a present for his cousin but forgotten Gokalp.

The last year of his elementary education, as far as he remembered, was an uneventful occasion. He remembers this mostly for being made to trace maps of the world on greaseproof paper, or standing in for teachers and taking the classes himself. It was also his teacher's last year in charge of the elementary school as he was to be the headmaster of the new Lycee that was to open.

Gokalp looked forward to going to the new school and was most anxious to start his secondary education there.

★ ★ ★ ★ ★

His father's drinking had grown less by then. It was noticeable for he would spend time at home. He would drink for a few days in moderation and then abstain for several weeks. Things were suddenly better. He had even taken out his mandolin to play. He was good at it but not patient enough to teach his son who wanted to learn to play.

Indeed, it had been very pleasant to see his father sober. They had even gone to the beach as a family a couple of times. They sat in the holes worn out of the rocks by stones trapped inside and made sandcastles and drew shapes of things on the sand. They would have their lunch of bread, cheese, tomato, cucumber, dolmas and watermelon, and return home in the late afternoon. But this was not to last.

One day as the time grew near for the new school to open he had to ask his father for the money to buy his books. It was not then the custom to buy new ones but to purchase old ones from a boy going on to a higher class who had himself bought them from someone else. New books were a luxury only a very few could afford. He had found someone who wanted to sell. The pages of the books were torn and worn in places, but the price of one pound ten shillings was the cheapest one could pay. This was a lot of money in those days.

His father suddenly started shouting at him and abusing him, saying all manner of things. The only thing he heard and kept on repeating were the words:

"I will not pay one pound ten shillings for you to buy books. I don't want you to go to school. I refuse to send you. I am going to take you and put you to work tomorrow."

He did not know whether or not his father had been drinking but all this had been heard by every neighbour and someone had sent for his grandmother. By the time she arrived the whole neighbourhood knew the reason for the upheaval.

She took control of the situation, saying that if that was how it was going to be, then there was nothing more to be said and better the thing was closed. He had seen his grandmother signal him to be quiet as she came through the door into the courtyard while unveiling herself.

That evening he had spent at his grandmother's, fearing the recurrence of the incident again that night.

The next morning he saw his grandmother take from the bottom of a clothes trunk, wrapped inside a large scarf, some old papers written in ancient Turkish script with stamps and seals on them. She looked at them then wrapped them up again and put them back. Two days later she gave him one pound ten shillings and a pair of new shoes.

He bought the books and glued the torn pages together with glue taken from Yorgo the cobbler. He rebound them in brown paper in the carpenter's shop where he used the vice to press the covers.

He was proud and very happy, for he had books that looked like new and would last. He hid his books on top of the clothes cabinet in his parent's bedroom, in his old school bag.

One lunch time, returning home from helping his grandfather in the market place he saw his mother sitting at the window of her room, his younger brother and the three sisters were on the floor playing and the baby in the bed sucking a dummy.

What they were playing with were his newly

rebound books and these were torn. He cried out to her, "Mother look what you let them play with! Don't you know they are my new school books?"

In his anger and shock he looked at his mother and saw her for the first time as someone who cared less or understood not what those books signified to him. He then looked at his brother who was only sixteen months younger than himself. He saw his brother look back at him and at the same time deliberately tear the pages of the book. He went for his brother.

When he had done with his brother and straightened himself to gather up his books he felt, then saw, a skewer sticking out of his back on the side of his spine just above his hip. He looked at his mother and saw the horror on her face. She stood there with her hand over her open mouth. She had thrown the skewer without a thought.

He pulled it out and rushed to his paternal aunt's house, whose husband was a doctor. The uncle by marriage, Dr. Ihsan Ali, saw to his needs and told him he was lucky that the skewer had not reached his kidney. All that he would have was a stiff back for a few days.

When he returned home his father was already there with both grandmothers and grandfathers. He asked him what had taken place. Before he had given his version of events up to the point where he saw his brother tear the pages, his father attacked him.

Had it not been for both his grandparents interfering, he would have suffered some permanent physical damage. What he did suffer was far worse.

★★★★★

The start of his secondary education seemed to him to be a continuation of his elementary schooling for he was set to tracing more world maps and maps of Turkey. They were to be used in classes where there was a shortage of materials. His companion at this task was Guner, son of Ali seller of buns. They became very close and their friendship developed. The two of them were at the top of the class.

★★★★★

Just before dawn one morning in early September 1953 the earth rumbled and shook for a few seconds.

The citizens of Paphos had always lived under the shadow of their fear of earthquakes. This ancient centre of civilisation had once been destroyed by an earthquake. There is a dread of earthquakes in every Paphian.

Gokalp was shaken out of sleep that morning. He jumped from his bed and ran to the next room where he took two of his sisters, one under each arm, out of the house. The older ones did what he told them and ran to the garden.

Grandfather Hüseyin Remzi Mehmed. Picture taken before his death in 1960.

Uncle Kemal with his great-uncle Hasan (Ziziri) sitting on a chair. Picture taken 22.6.1938.

Great-grandmother Safiye. Picture taken before 1950.

Circumcision ceremony memorial photograph.
Topline from left to right: Uncle Kemal, Sureya, İbrahim the circumciser, Kemal a cousin of Gökalp's father, and Gökalp's father.
Middle line: Saydam, cousin Savaş, Gökalp's younger brother, Gökalp and cousin Metin.
Lower line: Salih a cousin of Gökalp's father, Gökalp's sister Tulen, Faruk and Gökalp's sister Tumer.

Gökal and Metin in front of the wooden stairs.

The Jetty at Lower Paphos.

He was about to go back into the house when his mother came out with the baby saying:

"Oh my God. This is an earthquake. It will be the end of the world.....The end of the world has come!"

That is when he saw a large hole in the ground by the side of the door. A two metre deep perfectly rectangular well appeared where no one had ever thought one to exist.

Thus began life in tents which lasted for nearly two years. Occasional tremors shook the ground and people were afraid to step indoors, particularly those whose houses had been dangerously damaged or destroyed by the first wave.

Houses which were too dangerous to live in were pulled down by caterpillar tractors or bulldozers. For the times were changing.

The hydrogen bomb was exploded in the Pacific by the Americans. In Egypt the Arabs were in revolt. And Queen Elizabeth II had come to the throne of England. Britain had exploded its first atomic device, becoming the third power to do so. And there was talk that the Americans would drop an atomic bomb in Korea.

In Cyprus too, changes were taking place. Since 1947 people of the Orthodox faith had been allowed to settle on the Island from places as far away as Rumania,

Bulgaria, Egypt, Syria and Turkey.

They came and built new houses. They brought new trades and crafts and machinery, such as sewing machines that stitched leather and made shoes, lathes that worked by pulley and belt which the carpenters used instead of a bow and string pulled by hand to turn the wood, to be shaped into the leg of a table or chair, or a spinning top for the boys to play with.

Tractors replaced oxen, threshing of wheat was done by machines and water wheels stopped turning in their places. Perkins diesel engines came into use, tap water and electricity came to homes and houses were built of cement and baked bricks instead of by the four thousand year old techniques of mud bricks dried in the sun, set over a stone foundation.

* * * * *

Gokalp's next year at school began in tents. The tents were set up in what was the old Turkish cemetery of Paphos. And for the first time he had a teacher who was English, an old man who came from Egypt.

Frederick Victor Colonel was an upright, not so tall, white haired, pink-faced man with a slight pot-belly. He had retired from the Army with the rank of colonel and had been a teacher in Egypt before coming to Cyprus. He was a man of infinite patience. He had been a bachelor all his life. He came from somewhere along the coast of the Bristol Channel which he declared to be the most beautiful place on earth and that he would end his days there in retirement. But he also loved the desert.

Frederick Victor Colonel would say:

"I am a bachelor twice and a colonel twice. I am a bachelor of Arts and a bachelor in life. Also Colonel in name as well as rank."

Gokalp remembered him walking into the tent on his first day as their new English teacher. Although he had been learning English for the past three years he did not understand anything at all in that first class and nor did anyone else, apart from "This is a book", "This is a pen", "I am a teacher". But by the end of the year he had improved a lot.

* * * * *

That summer he had his first paid work.

The previous summer he had helped his grandfather in the market in the morning and before closing time at 1 pm. Around eleven or twelve o'clock he would take baskets of fruit into the open market in the street and sell them, usually on a commission from his grandfather. This was his paternal grandfather Dervis. In that way he had his pocket money. Then at one o'clock he would run to the beach with some fruit for lunch and stay there the rest of the day, swimming and lying in the sun.

He had also worked on a ship, unloading fertilisers on to barges out beyond the breakwater. This job came to him through the merchant Stephani, whose warehouses were by the mosque but the entrance to which office was by the bar where Gokalp's father did some of his drinking. For two day's work he got paid one pound and five shillings. It was a lot of money and all he did to earn it was to stand on an upper deck of the cargo ship and count the sacks, lifted from the hold by a crane and loaded onto the barges, and record the total. This was his first real paid job. This he did again when the next ship called at the port.

That summer his pay was one pound two shillings and sixpence a week and the job lasted him until the school opened.

He had applied for a job at the Public Works Department and with the help of his paternal uncle Ertugrul who worked at the central office, he got the job. He had the required qualifications. He could add, read and write in both Greek and Turkish and his knowledge of the English language was better than most.

At first he did the time keeping at different sites where the Public Works Department were building earthquake-proof houses in place of those destroyed. Before work started in the morning he was picked up by a lorry together with other workmen. At the site he would check the names of those present against his list and log the time. He checked them again before noon, after their midday meal and at the finish of the day. Once a week he submitted to the office the pay sheet that he had prepared. The workmen were mostly Greeks. The foreman who was responsible for the whole gang of around thirty was a round-faced big built giant of a man who had learned his trade from boyhood, working with his father. He had no schooling and could barely sign his name; he was a softly spoken quiet person, who never got cross with any of the workmen.

Within a short time Gokalp also found himself in charge of stores, at Lower Paphos, not far from the harbour; keeping stock of the distribution of materials. He was good at his work and enjoyed the responsibility. When discrepancies appeared at a different place under another foreman, he was sent there for a few days on loan by his own foreman as a favour to sort things out. This he did and the other foreman wanted to keep him for good. But he returned to his original place of work.

Within a week of this incident an inspector came and talked to the foreman. He knew by the way they glanced at him, although they were some distance away, that something was wrong. The foreman's face showed anger for the first time ever. They talked for quite a while. Finally the foreman slowly walked towards him.

When he stood in front of him, his face showed sorrow and he said:

"Somebody complained that you are not old enough

to work. I have been told to send you straight home. I do not want to but I have to do it. Now, listen carefully. Go now; tomorrow morning be at the usual place. I will speak to you then." Gokalp liked his work and had enjoyed the responsibility which was entrusted to him by the illiterate foreman builder. He had carried his duties through well. He was sorry it had to end like this. Next morning Gokalp was told to write labourer insted of time-keeper storeman on the time sheet and so was able to continue until the schools opened.

The trust which his foreman held in him at work and the financial benefit gained from it gave Gokalp a boost in his self confidence.

While working in Lower Paphos he took the opportunity and visited in his spare time, the Roman baths, the burial caves, the tombs of the Kings and the Pillar on which St. Paul was strapped and lashed. Near by he visited the tekke of the Lala of Mehmed Bey (Lala Mehmed Tekkesi). Tekke is a place for learning, study, Lala is a tutor, and Bey is rince. There at the Tekke he saw Roman type oil lamps still in use. At Old Paphos and Paphos thousands of years of history lay everywhere like an open book to be read and more was buried beneath the soil like pages to be turned over. He developed an interest in the history of his birth place.

This interest was further aroused when a French expedition unearthed Chalcolithic burial chambers in a field beyond the garden wall of their house. The skeletons discovered belonged to children and grown ups. They lay buried beneath the soil for thousands of years to be discovered and studied by people who came from a far away country.

He wanted to work there in the afternoons after school. He spoke to the French professor in charge who agreed to have him help. His pay was negotiated at a shilling a day. He told this to his father. He wished he hadn't. His father's attitude and words were, "Do you have nothing else to do except dig graves? No, I won't allow you to go and help". He was sorry to have asked his father. He vowed to himself never again to ask anything from his father, ever.

* * * * *

Gokalp was always taken to be older than his age. He had grown quite tall, taller in fact than all his class and than most of the older boys at school. He was slim but muscular. With his swimming and other sporting activities he developed muscles instead of fat. In the summer he would swim every day; in winter he would go for runs, play football and take part in school athletics.

With the money he earned he bought himself a watch and had his first suit made for him with long trousers, for until then he had worn his father's discarded police shorts, taken in. The money left over from these purchases was enough to last him for some time.

At school that year he gave himself up to his studies

and in particular to the learning of English. He would spend every available moment talking to his English teacher who he always addressed as "sir". They would walk and talk during breaks between classes and in the afternoons at the sports ground. Frederick Victor Colonel gave him books on loan to read.

★ ★ ★ ★ ★

His uncle by marriage, Doctor Ihsan, had built himself a new house, near to the residence of the District Commissioner, on the outskirts of the town on the road to Yeroshipru. Gokalp had taken to going there some afternoons to study and to read the especially delivered newspapers from Turkey and to make use of the books available at his uncle's library. He, in particular, remembered walking there one Sunday afternoon wearing for the first time the two visible evidences to his industry: his new suit and a brand new watch, his pride acquisition, radiant with self confidence and as carefree as any teenager in town.

In the summer months every day but especially on Sundays the people of the town would gather late in the afternoon on the triangle in the front of the police station and the cinemas. They would sit at cafes and patisseries in the open, watching people go by, the Greeks at their own cafes, the Turks at theirs. Only at the patisseries they would sit side by side. Then just before the sunset they would walk from the triangle past the police station on the left and the mock of a temple that was the municipal building, on the right, with the new fountains in the garden in front of it; on past the Greek elementary school, on the left, with its gabled facade. Next to the Greek elementary school stood the newly completed entrance to the gymnasium. This separated the elementary school from the Greek Lyceum. Opposite these stood the municipal gardens. They would continue past these and the newly opened "New Olympus" hotel and beyond his aunt's house, which stood just short of the bend in the road leading to the District Commissioner's residence. They would return by the same route, in twos, threes or larger groups, greeting and talking to each other, exchanging pleasantries and news. The young would eye each other, be they Greek or Turk, exchange glances or words, usually with the boys walking behind the girls of their fancy. An occasional passing landau, its tiny brass bells ringing to the beat of the trotting hooves of the horses, adding music to the air, moved them to the side; giving the right of way to its aloof occupants and colour to the conversation of the peripadists. So the young amused themselves and the older generation who had seen and lived it all. They were there to see and to be seen.

This was the style of the town. It was their way of life and it was a good life.

In previous years people of means would hire the landaus which stood parked in front of the hotel by the triangle, or call for one of these to take them from their homes, along the same route beyond the District

Commissioner's residence, over the small stone bridge to the village of Yeroshipru. There they would buy lokum - Turkish Delight. He remembered going on a trip such as this with his cousins and aunt, the doctor's wife. But by this time the car had replaced the landau at Paphos.

Like most young men of his age or a bit older he began to meet his friends in front of the cinema or on the corner opposite the patisserie, and to enjoy the walk. He considered himself to be old enough for this. After all, he was wearing long trousers!

The girls of his age were no longer silly creatures who whispered into each other's ears and giggled. He was growing up. He was becoming aware of the opposite sex.

That summer he noticed one particular girl for the first time, on the beach with her friends, playing and swimming. He had seen her before at the house next to his aunt's coming out onto the terrace, and she had seen him on his aunt's terrace many times, reading or studying or talking with his cousins. They had looked at each other from one terrace to the other.

He had watched her walk to the edge of the little pier built on the rocks of the municipal beach and had observed her perfectly shaped body, beautifully tanned skin and hazelnut-coloured thick hair down to her shoulders. She looked absolutely beautiful. There, looking at her from the rocks, he saw her dive into the water and swim to the raft. He watched her all the way, saw her climb onto the raft, pull her hair back behind her neck with both hands then dive in again and swim back. As she drew near he saw her big, wide eyes looking at him. She was swimming towards him instead of towards the pier.

As she climbed out of the water he thought of her as Aphrodite reborn.

He was not the only one observing her. Just then one of his friends called out to him from behind and he turned back. Then there were shouts and much splashing. When he looked again he saw that some of the boys, including one of his friends, Venhar, who had been standing just below him to the side on the rocks, had jumped into the water to pull her out because she had put her foot on a sea urchin and was in considerable pain.

Her friends were by her side by then. He heard her ask one of them who had rescued her, and when she pointed to this boy, he heard her say:

"I wish it had been the other one," looking at Gokalp.

"But he is a Turk," said her friend

"I don't care," she replied.

Gokalp felt a twinge of jealousy, for in his heart he wanted to be the boy who had lifted her out of the water.

So started their innocent puberty love, she fearlessly declaring her emotions, he secretly wishing he had been the one who rescued her.

That evening on the way to his aunt's house he saw her taking a stroll with her friends. She had her foot bandaged and was supported by the girl who had earlier in the day objected to Gokalp for being a Turk. He stopped and talked to her for the first time. He asked after her injured foot and she said she was fine and hoped to see him on the beach the next day. They parted with Gokalp saying he would be there.

He could hear her friends speaking angrily to her as he walked away. He glanced back and their eyes met: at that moment time stood still for him. For the first time he felt elevated in a new kind of excitement and at the same time felt a twinge of jealousy for not being the one to have lifted her out of the water. They saw each other on the beach and on their afternoon walks. Always they had friends with them. He learned that she took piano lessons from a German woman living near the hospital and that after her lessons her friends came to meet her and together they all went to visit their other friend living next to his aunt's house; his paternal aunt Mebrure, the doctor's wife. So Gokalp took to waiting with his cousin Savas, whenever possible, and school activities permitting, at the school library, which was at the top of the school's football field, from where they could observe the hospital and the German woman's small wooden house. And when they saw her come out and was met by her friends he and Savas would hurry to reach them, pretending it was a well met coincidence. So they walked a few paces behind them down the road running from the hospital to the municipal gardens, the only road at Paphos lined with pine trees on both sides of the road, parasols giving shade where the air was redolent with the smell of pine. At the end of the road they would pass the girls and walk ahead. Etiquette dictated that. For it was accepted that boys walked faster than girls.

★ ★ ★ ★ ★

So passed the last innocent summer for the children of Paphos, the descendants of Aphrodite, the Paphian goddess of Love, Peace and Happiness, unaware that other gods and goddesses and, indeed, immortal men such as the Archbishop of Cyprus and the King of Greece together with the lesser immortals, the politicians and the higher echelons of the army of Greece, were waiting in the wings to have a hand in the destiny of the lives of the peoples of the Island of Cyprus and its history. For, this was decreed by higher immortals, the Phil-Helen politicians of the 19th century England, France and Russia, who created the Helen nation which is represented by the modern Greek state today, and wrote it's history with no other object in mind other than to have a mandatory "Greek" state with claims, historic claims on the empire and the civilisation of the Roman people and on lands where others had lived for thousands of years, to serve their political ends then.

For, it was in that year, in 1954, that Greece brought the Cyprus issue up at the United Nations. It claimed historical right to the island and demanded from the United Nations the sovereignty of the island be taken from the British Crown - the island had been a British Crown colony since 1925 - and given to the Greek Crown as if people and provinces could be bartered from sovereignty to sovereignty on claimed historical right of a nation six hundred miles away across the sea that had itself come into being as a geographical and political entity on the world map only 124 years earlier in 1830.

But the political conjecture and the political map of the world had changed since the writing of the Greek history in the 19th century for political ends or the European mandatory powers. And the Greek politicians being too much immersed in and impressed with the past history of their achievements probably had no time to realise this truth.

As in the Iliad, the epic poem attributed to Homer and to the Greeks (Iliad is not Greek, discoveries at Ugarit put it firmly to a Middle Eastern origin), it was in that year, in 1954, that the goddess Discord did throw, again, her golden apple, the same apple she had thrown at the nuptials of Peleus and Thetis the parents of Achiles, with the inscription "for the fairest"; and Athena the goddess of war, destruction and perdition who saw herself as the fairest, or rather the politicians and the higher echelons of the army of modern Greece - all of them indoctrinated with the past glories and heroic acts of the ancient citizens of a city state where Athena was worshipped - prepared to enter the contest despite Hera, modern Turkey, to rob Aphrodite, Cyprus, of her title.

Athena who was also reputed to have been the goddess of wisdom did, as she had in ancient times, a foolish thing. The conflict of gods in the twentieth century was to be re-enacted not at Troy but in the island of Cyprus.

None of the Greek government's demands at United Nations concerned Gokalp. He did not believe, nor did anyone of the Turkish population of the island of Cyprus, that Great Britain would relinquish its rule over Cyprus. Not even the old men who sat all day at cafes and talked nothing but politics, who were sincere in their belief and saw themselves adept at solving world problems, who talked about Mustafa Kemal and Venizelos as if they were alive and Alexander the Great and Husrev (Xerxes) as someone who had passed through history yesterday, were much concerned with the Greek government's demands at United Nations. At Paphos, at Turkish cafes and at homes, politics was something which occupied old men, grandfathers, great uncles and aunts who were educated under the Ottoman system, who lived to see the change at the end of the First World War - the demise of the Ottoman empire and Caliphate in 1924 - and to become identified with the modern Turkish republic, and now to be witnesses to the demands of the Greek government six hundred miles away across the sea whereas from the northern shoreline of the island of Cyprus the land-mass of Turkey forty miles away was visible to the naked eye. And if ever Britain relinquished it's authority over Cyprus, the Cypriot Turks expected the island to revert to Turkish rule, as stated in Lausanne Agreement of 1923, which gave the geographical borders and political recognition to Turks on the map of the world.

Gokalp's concern was for his future. For the first time his mind was occupied by thoughts of what he would become. He had started to ask himself "what will become of me?" Searching for a direction for his life ahead he had asked his grandmother, when she told him that everyone had written on the forehead his or her future at birth and nothing could change that, if he could know now what the future had held for him. Her answer had been "it will be what is written". And yet in the year of the Queen's coronation, the year in which they laid pipes to bring tap water to houses at Paphos, he had stopped to watch the testing and cleaning of the water pipes to see the jet of water come down as rain to form a rainbow, and had remembered then the one particular occasion with his grandmother at Musalla, which was an open air mosque on high ground attended only at the end of the holy month of Ramadan to celebrate the Ide of Ramadan, from where they had seen the most spectacular rainbow ever over the rock-hewn tombs of the kings. He had reminded her then of one of her stories in which a young and handsome man who catches the rainbow, which becomes his coat, and has all the riches of the world at his feet. In his childish mind he would have liked to have reached to catch the rainbow there and then; and had told her so; but knew it even then to be impossible. But the rainbow formed by the spray of the jet of water was within his reach. Knowingly he had reached to catch it then, only to have his hand wet. He remembered going home and telling this to his grandmother. "One day you will catch the rainbow", she had said to him. He wondered if what she had said, then, would come to pass. Until then would he come to chase rainbows?

Well, what was it going to be? He had thought of and had asked himself that question many times. The only thing he could imagine for himself under the circumstances was that he might perhaps go to the Teacher Training college and eventually become a teacher himself. But he could not see his father ever agreeing to that. It would entail two years further education at the College after leaving school and such higher education would, he knew, even though it was part state subsidised, be out of the question because of the expense. He could not communicate with his father. He was afraid to do so.

By now the family had increased. The children numbered eight in all, four boys and four girls and yet again his mother was expecting a baby. What could he expect from his parents?

He had heard of people going to far-away countries, to England and Australia to become rich, far-away places like China and places in Africa returning to build themselves new houses to live in, like the one beyond the post office on the way to the old port opposite the fountain, with Chinese characters set on the pavement, in cement, leading to its porch.

He had dreams of going to these far-away lands to work and make a fortune. He could certainly then build himself a new house. But if he had a choice what would he have preferred to be? A teacher, a doctor, an architect, an accountant, a merchant or go away to far-off lands to seek his fortune? In his dreams he could see himself as an architect building houses and one for himself, as a teacher, as a doctor even as a soldier and a pilot. His father had made fun of him when he let it be known that he nursed ambition of becoming a pilot. But the thought of going away to far off-places and returning back rich excited him most.

As his secret thoughts and aspirations went through his mind he looked also at the lack of opportunities at hand to realise any of his ambitions and felt insecure. His friends whose fathers were tradesmen or those who had only one brother or sister had no problems as to how to pay for their higher education or how to arrange their future. Some had already left to go to better schools in Nicosia or Famagusta as did his cousin Metin, the son of his maternal uncle Kemal who was running the farm. Even Ulku, the daughter of his aunt, was attending the church school run by sisters of Terra Santa at Nicosia. He became aware of what was reality and attainable. What he thought would be best for him, under the circumstances, was to work with his grandfather in the market place and possibly take over from him when he retired or died. To him this was his best chance, the only opportunity open to his future well being; therefore education seemed unnecessary and futile.

* * * * *

Yet, he acquired the knowledge available from books and from his teachers without conscious effort. He was punished and even suspended together with Guner from classes for a few days for insolence. That is until their hair grew to an acceptable length. The two of them had gone and shaved their Tony Curtis hair style because the headmaster at the morning assembly had made a remark in general about the length of hair sported by boys. The two like-minded friends decided there and then to go and shave their head hair that very afternoon to show their protests. At the assembly next morning the headmaster accepted that Tony Curtis hairstyles were better that a large shiny egg over shoulders. They were sent home after their form master objected to their presence in class.

The Headmaster, who had been his teacher at Elementary school, always showed him tolerance.

But he was the favourite with the history teacher, with the Turkish Literature teacher, and, of course, with his English teacher.

His history teacher would lower his marks on examination papers, telling him that he would have received full marks had it not been for writing more answers than the questions required according to the books, and producing his own thoughts and opinions as to the events in history.

So it was with Turkish literature, but in spite of his being sent off for a few days from school, the speech he wrote for Youth and Sports Day, a national day held on 19th May, was chosen by his form master Harid Fedai to be the one good enough to be delivered, by Gokalp, on that day to the assembled school and parents at the sports ground.

But it was from "Sir", his English teacher, Frederick Victor Colonel, that he learned most in their talks together. One day they were debating a certain subject as they walked in the yard and his teacher's advice to him became his maxim from then on. It was as follows:

"If you want to talk on any subject with authority, first you must read as many books with diverse views on it as you can. Then, when you have done this, you can speak with authority and conviction".

"Sir" shaped his way of thinking, while the others merely wanted from him an unquestioning, dogmatic acceptance and conformity.

* * * * *

He conformed to life's demands. He helped his grandfather whenever he could, usually on Saturday mornings.

At home things were the same as before but now he would send his sister to the provision merchant with the book in her hand in the mornings. He still polished his father's boots. His mother sometimes got up early with morning sickness. His younger brother now fought with every boy in the street.

He would see Maro on the terrace from his aunt's house after her piano lessons and at the municipal gardens where he went with his cousin to watch people playing tennis. At other times on his way to his aunt's house he would, by way of a detour, pass her house. Sometimes she would be reading at other times she would be combing her hair at her window.

Then on 25th January 1955 six Greeks from mainland Greece and seven Cypriots were caught landing arms and explosives from a fishing boat in a cove at Paphos. He first knew of this from his father. His father was one of the policeman who took part in the operation at the village of Hloraka.

After this no one wondered or had any doubt as to what the Greeks were preparing for. They were arming themselves for a bloody struggle.

In February on the day of the preliminary hearing for the accused gun runners there were demonstrations outside the court house. Gokalp had stood by and watched the demonstrators. He had gone to the Court house hoping to see Rauf Denktas, the Paphian born Turkish Cypriot Public Prosecutor, who had married the granddaughter of one of the distant cousins of Gokalp's great grandmother Safiye. There was talk then that Rauf Denktas, the Chief Public Prosecutor, would present the case against the accused.

So it was a few days before the preliminary hearing that the new school building was opened. It stood by the Police station separated from the Greek Gymnasium by a road. His class was moved from the house near the Bishop's residence to the first floor of the new building.

Then in the middle of March when the court sat to hear the case brought against the arms smugglers again there were disturbances. This time stones were thrown at the court house and windows were broken. The demonstration went on daily attracting larger crowds.

By now the topic of every conversation among the older people was of the impending troubles. But none could guess when that would be or what form they would take. This was the prevailing uncertainty in which the people lived and it was in this atmosphere that he was sent to Nicosia to stay with his cousin Elvan while her husband was away, unaware of what fate held in hand for him.

Fate, the goddess, in her power had predetermined events unalterably for eternity was watching her players at their role at the early minutes on 1st April 1955. Gokalp was fast sleep. He was to be woken up by the sound of bombs.

That is how the arrival of EOKA was heralded for him by the sound of bombs. Posters were stuck on the walls by terrorists to announce the birth of EOKA and to proclaim the name of its leader Dighenis, the mythological hero of the Greek people. He was none other than Colonel George Grivas, himself a Cypriot, who had lived and fought in Greece during the Civil War. He had landed secretly in Cyprus and set up his undercover organisations by the direct order of Archbishop Makarios.

On his return, at first, things seemed normal at Paphos. No bombs had yet exploded there. People took their afternoon walks and gathered around the triangle. Policemen still sat in the shade of an apricot tree at the immaculately kept gardens in front of the police station to have a break, to pass away a few leisurely minutes, to have a coffee, a cigarette. Only the previous year he remembered sitting there with Tuncay, who had come to spend her holidays at Paphos, to wait for his father to take them with him in the police jeep to Lower Paphos to swim by the jetty where his father instructed other policemen in life saving. He remembered the occasion when father was rushed to Lower Paphos to save the life of a drowning man. Father had no time to collect his swimming trunks. He undressed in the jeep while being driven and dived into water with his underpants which came off and were lost. It was there while taking a leisurely break under the apricot tree that Sergeant Abdullah jumped over the wall and ran after a fellow named Andrea Zembilo, who was pushing a bicycle and carrying a violin case which contained a Sten gun, shouting at him to stop.

But it was inevitable that things would change and gatherings would become demonstrations, walks protest marches.

One evening a terrorist walked into a bar near the municipal gardens, towards Musalla, and shot dead a man named Gannavuro. Gannavuro was playing poker with Mustafa, son of Altıbarmak (Sixfingers). He was killed because he did not heed the advise of EOKA to end his frienship with his Turkish cronies. Mustafa who had been threatened with a beating, or a fate similar to Gannavuro's, never ventured to visit this place after his experience. Then one day a bomb was thrown at a military Land Rover, on a patrol going down to Lower Paphos, from somewhere below Musalla. When he heard the explosion and the shots which followed, Gokalp was up on an almond tree in the garden with a basket gathering almonds. A British soldier, a sergeant, was dead, his guts blown out by the bomb; his father told him that when he came home. Later that night one of the Greek boys living at the top of the road took to the hills as a wanted man and as a member of the terrorist organisation. That is how EOKA showed its presence in Paphos.

The beautiful stone building of the police station gradually became a fortress. First the shutters were closed against stone throwing, then wire mesh was put over them. Observer posts were built at the back and some of the windows in front were used for the same purpose after being protected with sandbags. Barbed wire barricades were erected blocking the entrance to it and the street.

His father started carrying a pistol. Armed British soldiers appeared at the police station, manning the observer posts.

Despite all this life went on as before for old man Midas who still plied his trade carrying his by now antique air gun and the wooden board with circular targets around the stone water tank or by a tall cypress tree near the police station for boys to practice shooting, three shots for a penny. No one told Midas not to.

★ ★ ★ ★ ★

Coming of warm weather brought with it an increase in demonstrations and in acts of terrorism all over the island. News would reach Paphos, the most isolated part of the island, and its Greek young would go to task to prove themselves more nationalistic than the rest. And there appeared, then, older boys in Maro's group of friends. He was to learn later that these boys who looked at him with eyes that could kill planned to give Gokalp a good beating up.

The triangle became the proving ground for the demonstrating Greek youth. And the Turks stood by and watched as spectators to the developments.

Gokalp found himself in groups with his friends and with his teachers, talking of the Greek Cypriot demand for union with Greece and what that implied to the Turks of the island; that they could never accept. British rule was acceptable and was seen as the best solution until the leaders of the Turkish community announced their view: "Cyprus is Turkish".

Gokalp began to talk to his teachers about organising some kind of demonstrations to bring it home to the authority that they themselves, the Turkish Cypriots, had their own point of view. They had to make their presence felt on the island.

At first the attitude of the teachers was: "we must not..." then it became "we cannot..." This did not deter Gokalp. Then finally as the Youth and Sports day of 19th May neared, one afternoon during rehearsals for this he approached his teacher Ali Suha again. This time he told Ali Suha there was the opportunity for them to show themselves in force. He reasoned why shouldn't they assemble at the house next to the Bishop's residence in the Greek quarter of the town and march past the Greek stronghold to the sports ground. "You have to have permission from the District Commissioner to do that." His teacher had replied. This was his chance and he jumped at it. He told his teacher he would get the permission from Mr Williams. If he did this his teacher told him then they would go along with his plans.

That afternoon Gokalp went to see Mr. Williams the District Commissioner at his residence near his aunt's house. He was taken by a secretary into a room and offered some lemonade. After a few minutes, Mr. Williams, who he knew by sight, came in.

Gokalp stood up and introduced himself by his full name. He stated his school and in which class he was, he also said that he was a nephew of the Commissioner's neighbour, the doctor, who was a leader of the Turkish Cypriot community.

Mr. Williams listened to all this and then, telling him to sit down asked him why he had come.

Gokalp told him he wanted permission to assemble at the house near the bishop's residence, which was still part of the school although unused, and to march from there in front of the Greek schools, past the municipal building by the police station and the triangle, turn right by the patisserie, and so come to the sports ground. All the marchers were to be from the school and would be accompanied by their teachers.

Mr. Williams asked if the procession would be orderly and peaceful and if flags were to be carried. Gokalp assured him it will be peaceful and that there would be just one flag.

Next day when he presented himself on the appointed hour at the District Commissioner's office Mr.

Williams personally told him that permission was granted.

He was not surprised at all. In his boyish innocence he had no doubts at all, not even for one moment, that permission could or would be withheld. Excited he went to work. He had only two days to get things organised.

Up to then on Sports Day those taking part wore white shorts, sweatshirts and tennis shoes. The rest of the school usually watched the parade around the sports ground, which was a football pitch with a hard surface, in their ordinary school uniforms, together with some of the parents, standing under the enormous pine tree or in the shade of carob trees. It was an extra expense for most of the families to fit their children out with a sports outfit. Those taking part assembled in the building at the top of the ground. They then marched down the side of the ground, past the goal posts, and back by the other side.

As he could not get everybody to wear white shorts, tennis shoes and sweatshirts, the rest of the pupils were arranged in a motley collection of school uniforms and hats. They all practised for two days how to march: Left - Right - left - right: one - two - three - four: Left - right - left. He would have very much liked to have had them drilled the way a Greek teacher did accross the road at the Greek Cymnasium sports field.

Grandfather Huseyin's youngest brother İbrahim Hakkı Mehmet (standing at the back) with his cousin Sultan (left) and her father Celal Hursit, an uncle by marriage with Sultan's half sister Zehra (on her father's lap).

Gökalp's teachers. School year 1953-54.
From left to right kneeling: Selim Hoca, Yusuf Öztürk.
Standing: Ali Suha, Ömer Halis Eşmeli, Burhan Demir, Harid Fedai and Frederick Victor Colonel.

On a school auting at Trodos mountains, 5th March 1954. From left to right: Güner Ali with hair grown to an acceptable langth Zeynel, Oztan and Yalçın Faik the tallest boy at school.
Standing: Necati Taşkın (Samişari), Saydam Salih and a boy with a school cap.

At Lower Paphos 1955: Gökalp is on extreme left standing.

At Lower Paphos 1955: Gökalp with arms crossed, standing extreme right, Venhar is kneeling at the front.

At Lower Paphos 1955: This time in the middle of the girls.

Gökalp's mother when her children numbered 8 and the 9th on the way.

He marched in front of them, not, as he was supposed to do in the front line dressed in white, flanking the tallest boy at school who carried the flag. This was the day, 19th May 1955, which quietly saw the presence of Cypriot Turks at Paphos.

That day also he made a speech and his friend Guner read a poem. After this he changed into white and took part in the athletics, jumping through a bicycle wheel from which the spokes had been removed and padded with cotton soaked in paraffin, then set ablaze.

★★★★★

So life went on. Craftsmen toiled at their craft, tradesmen at their trade. At the market place people shopped at which ever, or whosever stall they found a bargain. Ethnic discrimination and hatred had not yet been decreed by the lesser immortals. In the late afternoon they still gathered around the triangle and if one did not demonstrate and the other watch they walked and then went to an open air cinema to see Marilyn Monro in Niagara, Sylvana Magnana in Bitter Rice, the "633 Squadron" or the "Life of Valentino" the greatest screen lover; James Stewart and John Wayne in cowboy films, Burt Lancaster, Tony Curtis and Gina Lollobrigida in the Greatest Show on Earth and then went home and slept with their windows wide open. People did not fear one another and the dread of EOKA had yet to come. But discreetly the seeds of hatred had been fostered in the young.

As he had done for many years on his way to school Gokalp passed every day down the street known as the street of prostitutes. The most famous resident of the street was Marulla, the aged high priestess of the purveyors of love for sale. Marulla ran one of the establishments there. In the morning on the way to school it was the most quiet street but come the afternoon Marulla would be sitting in her doorway and her girls in the hall in their Sunday best ready to sell their favours. There were other prostitutes in the same street but none was as famous as Marulla.

Towards the end of that summer for the first time Marulla, aware of his and his friends' adolescence, took to throwing complimentary remarks at them as they passed by in the early evening to go to the triangle or the cinema. At first they were amused by her remarks as to how tall they all have grown to be, how handsome they all looked, and how dearhearts they all have become. She was well-qualified and had the right as any in town to know and to make remarks; after all they all have been passing her door since their days of old, wearing shorts to go to school.

At first they were amused. They laughed and joked about her remarks amongst themselves. But then one day Marulla's psychology changed. She extended an invitation to initiate them into sexual delight with any one of her girls of their choosing. This invitation by the high priestess of the purveyors of love for sale at Paphos, a gift of Marulla's could not be lightly joked nor could it be snubbed. Some of the boys at school were talking about their experiences with the opposite sex at one or the other of the establishments. Gokalp and his friends had to put an end to their one-upmenship. They had to graduate to the class of the sexually experienced to avoid being rediculed as mere boys not yet matured. After all they were fifteen years old; at the age of maturity. So, seriously they discussed the subject and pondered upon the biggest danger, which was to be seen going in or coming out of her establishment by one of their teachers who lived a few doors away.

One evening on their way to the cinema they summoned up enough courage and seeing there was no one else in the street they went in. Here he had his first experience with a girl not much older than himself. Later at the cinema, having missed the beginning, he fell asleep from exhaustion and missed the rest of the "Life of Valentino" the greatest screen lover, which was the film that night at Aticon open air cinema.

An enlarged picture of Maro was put on display in the shop window of Spiro the photographer. He remembered stopping and looking at it. The last time he had seen her was at the municipal gardens where he had gone with his cousin Ulku, who was home for Christmas holidays, to watch people playing tennis. She happened to be there as well. The two girls who knew each other started to talk and he had out of politeness moved a few paces to the side to engage someone he knew in polite conversation. It was then that the ever present older boys in her group of friends appeared. Hurriedly his cousin Ulku came and told him that they must go away now. For the older boys were there to start a fight with intent to do him harm.

* * * * *

On the afternoon of Christmas eve a bomb was thrown at the British soldier manning the observation post at the back of the police station.

Gokalp was studying in the library of the new school building behind the police station. When he heard the explosion he was standing by the window, some eighty to one hundred yards from the observation post. He saw someone crouching behind the wall, at right angles to the Greek Gymnasium sports ground wall running the length of the street at the back of the police station, who ran to a bicycle parked by the bust of a Greek hero on the Greek Gymnasium sports ground. As the man reached the bicycle a Land Rover pulled up by the observation post. Gokalp called out to Sergeant Abdullah in the Land Rover that the man was now riding his bicycle towards the exit on the far side of the sports ground. "We will get him", said the sergeant and they did, as he came out of the exit onto the pine lined road running from the hospital to the municipal gardens.

Later that afternoon, Gokalp was taken to the police station to identify the man as the one he had seen at the time of the explosion. He felt no unease or excitement at being there in the courtyard of the station, waiting. He was familiar with the place and the policemen were no strangers to him. He had been there many times with his father before the troubles started and the building became a fortress. As he waited in the courtyard talking to a policeman a door to a cell was opened and he was able to see the man clearly and identify him by the way he was dressed and from the shape of his profile.

He was then taken to make a statement on the first floor offices in the presence of a captain. After he had done so he was taken out of the police station the same way he had come in, by the back door opening onto the side of his school.

He felt he had done his duty and thought nothing of it. At home he gave an account of the events to his mother. When this event took place Gokalp's father, demoted to the rank of corporal, was stationed at Athalasia, a training camp for police commandos outside Nicosia.

A few days later, on 11th January 1956, the police sergeant Abdullah, who was also a friend and a colleague of his father, was shot dead inside a carpenter's shop where he had been called in by the carpenter, a neighbour of the sergeant, under some pretext or other. The gunman who stood hidden behind the door shot the sergeant and ran out. But Sergeant Abdullah managed to hit the gunman with a shot, at the heel, before he collapsed.

When this happened Gokalp thought one day the same might befall his father. It never occurred to him that he himself would be next on the EOKA's death list.

* * * * *

Then, in March 1956, Archbishop Makarios was exiled to the Seychelles. This had euraged the Greek community and coused an increase in demonstrations against the British. Further, as the time neared it's first aniversary EOKA's acts of terror became by for the blodiest ever commited not only against the British serviceman but also against British civilians. For, they were shot in broad daylight in the streets of Nicosia and other towns. In Paphos too a British civilian was shot dead near the Ottoman Bank.

A few days after this, on a worm afternoon in early April, as Gokalp walked by Yanni's shop, Zehra Amber's father's shop next to Rex the patisserie on the corner to the triangle, another bomb exploded. This time it was thrown at the Auxiliary Police Headquarters which was housed on the first floor of the same building round the corner from the patisserie. He had seen someone come out of the unoccupied new building directly opposite the patisserie and join two man sitting outside at the cafe next door. There was no one else around. Gokalp was sure that this was the man who had thrown the bomb, although he did not see him do it. Gokalp thought their behaviour odd. A bomb had exploded a stone's throw away from them and they had not shown any curiosity or interest but sat as if nothing happened.

He walked across to the side of the road, a couple of passers-by, who thought they had been injured by flying glass, were quietly examining themselves. A silence prevailed over the scene for some seconds. One by one people started to gather and then to ask each other what had happened. They talked quietly at first, suddenly a couple of women came screaming out of the dry cleaner's shop walking over broken glass directly below the balcony where the bomb had exploded. One of them, a rounded woman, came to him and showed him a cut she had in her breast. He told her it was nothing but a scratch.

Then he saw an auxiliary policeman Ahmed come out of the building. The front of his khaki tunic open, his white sweat shirt stained red in blood. He walked unsteadily to the middle of the road, pulling at his sweat shirt with his blood-stained left hand. Gokalp rushed to him. He held the man steady. He lifted the man's torn sweat shirt and saw a deep gash on the right side of the body. He had smaller cuts above that and some in the face. "I am going to die, I am going to die, I know I am going to die", the man said in a whisper looking Gokalp in the eye. The man's face had turned white as chalk.

Gokalp knew the man who was a few years older than himself and, like most of the Turks, had joined the Auxiliary Police force for the sake of employment it offered.

Without a word Gokalp lifted the man in his arms. He felt the warm sticky blood on his own body as he hurried across the triangle to a taxi parked in front of the old hotel where the landaus had once stood. He got him into the taxi and told the driver to take them to the hospital.

From the hospital Gokalp went home to change his bloodstained clothes. He told his wondering mother what had happened and hurried back. This time by the patisserie he noticed some of the Greek boys sitting with one of their teachers, a mainland Greek, who had the bearing of a military man and who Gokalp had seen drilling boys from the Gymnasium under the pretence of athletic parades. They pointed him out as he was a few paces from their table. The teacher turned round and looked at Gokalp. Gokalp looked at them all in return. Further up in front of the police station other students were gathering in strength for a demonstration.

That night saw one of the biggest disturbances in Paphos and a curfew was declared.

* * * * *

The next day on his way home from helping his grandfather he was stopped by two men in front of the barber's shop. One of the men asked him if he was the son of the police sergeant. The man did not know him, he was sure of that. He knew he must have been pointed out to him by the barber. He had seen them standing together and looking at him as he walked up. Stavri the barber , had kept his eye on him until he was a few paces away from them and then had rushed into his shop.

The smaller of the two men said his friend wanted to talk to Gokalp. He spoke in Turkish. The other man, who had a permanent grin which showed his gold teeth, wore the baggy kilt and the peasant boots, did not say a word but kept grinning. Gokalp was puzzled as to what they wanted to talk to him about. He turned to the man with gold teeth and asked what it was all about. Without a change in his expression the man with the gold teeth started to talk in broken Turkish, saying that they knew his father and that he was a good man: and that they wanted Gokalp to testify in court and to the police that he was mistaken about the man he had seen crouch behind the wall and then run to the bicycle, and that the man he saw in the police station was not the same one who had the bicycle. If he did that they would be his friends.

His dignity hurt and incensed at the man's naked affront to his moral worth, he went home and told his mother what had happened. His uncle Kemal was sent for and he came from the farm. He told the whole story to his uncle who wanted to know how he had replied to the man's request. He answered that he would not think of doing as the two men wanted, and that he had told them so.

His uncle advised him to be careful when he was out of doors. He then went and talked to the stone breaker, the neighbour whose bedroom window was directly opposite the front door of the house in the narrow alleyway.

Some time before dawn in the dark hours of the next morning, two men knocked at the courtyard door of Gokalp's house. Before anyone in the house could reply, the neighbour called out from his window to ask who was there.

The answer came back that they were from the police station and that they had come to take the sergeant back with them as he was wanted there.

The stone cutter then told them that the sergeant was in Nicosia. When he opened the window he saw the backs of their uniforms as they rounded the corner of the alleyway.

That day a message was brought for him by his grandmother Saffet from her daughter, the doctor's wife who was his father's sister, to warn Gokalp that he should not visit them anymore as things were dangerous. His mother did not pass this message on to him.

So that is where he was when he last saw Maro.

He was inside the house, reading, when he heard the explosion. When he came out onto the terrace he saw four girls come out of the house next door in a state of great excitement; one of the four was Maro. He was looking at her when suddenly she turned and saw him there. She stood frozen in her tracks. Her expression on her face changed. She was seeing someone she was not supposed to or expected to see. One of her friends noticed this and pulled her by the hand. She walked the few steps down with them and turned and looked again. Their eyes met and the moment stood still for the last time for them. She then turned and walked away with her friends.

Someone had thrown an explosive device at the military Land Rover as it passed and it had gone off after the Land Rover had gone quite a distance. It had done no damage, not even a broken window, when it exploded at the side of the road right in front of the house of their neighbour.

He pondered many times as to who could have thrown it.

★ ★ ★ ★ ★

Gokalp was unaware that he was now on top of the death list drawn up by EOKA command. He had turned down their offer of friendship and refused to change his evidence. They had failed in their attempt to get into his house probably to frighten and intimidate him to change his evidence. The committee decided he should die.

The stone mason, the neighbour, first noticed a strange youth waiting, on the corner of the wood carver's shop, early one morning on his way to the quarry. Later he told his wife what he had noticed and asked her to be on the look out. The mason's wife, an adopted daughter to Gokalp's grandfather Huseyin's aunt, did what her husband asked. The next day on his way home the mason stopped to talk to a Greek he knew well to be connected with the terrorist organisation and asked them to think before they started to hurt the innocent boys and children of the neighbourhood. As fate would have it years later it was the mason's wife Zehra who suffered the worst. Her son Hassan, who was the same age as Gokalp, was made to kneel and then shot at the back of the head by a Greek officer in front of her in her front yard at the end of the alleyway.

Unaware also of the role the mason's wife had taken on, Gokalp was puzzled to see his mother up early in the mornings talking to the neighbours, at the entrance to the alleyway, when he left home to go to school. But they were there and they foiled the last attempt made to kill Gokalp at Paphos.

The strange youth was marked by them and when they noticed him that morning taking his position on the corner they marched up to him to challenge him. When one of the women noticed the gun on him she screamed "He has a gun, he is the killer". Faced with a bunch of screaming mothers the would-be killer had no choice but take to his heels.

Unknown to Gokalp, the court hearing was to be the next morning.

After lunch that day his friends Saydam, Venhar, Zeynel, Altan, Mustafa, Oztan and Guner called to see him. They pledged their friendship and loyalty to stand by him. In the garden under the almond tree they performed what was to them the most sacred ceremony. Each cut his own thumb and pressed it to the others mixing their blood. They then placed their hand on the knife and swore an oath to avenge should anything happen to either of them and licked the blood from the incision to become blood brothers.

Having done so they talked of becoming members of VOLKAN the Turkish secret organisation they had heard of. They were so carried away in their boyish enthusiasm that by the time they parted they had convinced themselves that they were VOLKAN. After all how many times before had they talked among themselves to organise into a defence unit?

* * * * *

It was soon after his friends had gone that the police came and told him not to go out of the house.

At sunset, loudspeakers on a Land Rover announced that a twenty-four hour curfew was declared henceforth. Everyone wondered what was happening. The hearsay was that a house-to-house search was going to take place.

A Land Rover with an armed escort came in the

morning to the front of his house, its engine running, it stood parked to the entrance to the alleyway. A sergeant came into the courtyard and told him he was to go court as a witness.

He climbed on the back of the waiting Land Rover. He looked up and down the street. It was empty and lifeless. He had never seen it like that before, silent and empty. Even the stray dogs had taken refuge somewhere. They drove the short distance to the court house, observing the silence, the sergeant in the front passenger seat and an auxiliary constable at the back, guns ready in their hands.

At the court house he was taken up to the first floor where he was kept waiting until he was called to give evidence. While waiting he thought of the empty streets he had passed to arrive here. Even the court house was empty and lifeless. The silence was eerie. He felt the same sensation as he had felt years ago when the rumbling and the shaking of earth had stopped and an eerie silence had prevailed until the howling of a dog nearby followed by others in the distance had broken it.

Here at the court house the silence was broken by the tiptoeing policemen going about their duty. They were ordered to do so by a captain who came out of the courtroom when they had first arrived there. The noise, the metal studs on their boots made on the tiled floor had carried to the far corner of the quiet court house.

The same captain came out and Gokalp was taken into the courtroom. He became aware of his own footsteps carrying in the solemn and almost empty courtroom. He had metal studs like the policemen on the heels and toes of his shoes. He took his place at the witness stand. He had been in this courtroom once before to hear a murder case on trial. At that time the courtroom was full, every seat occupied to capacity and the back was jammed with people standing up. At this hearing there were no spectators at all. Only the presiding judges, the prosecutor, the defending solicitor, himself and the policemen were present.

He took the oath to tell the truth, and looked across at the accused.

On the way back the sergeant was talkative, he told Gokalp that the highest judge was presiding over the case. He also said that the terrorist had had a paraffin test on his hand that had proved positive. When Gokalp asked what that was, it was explained to him that it was a test carried out to see if a person had used an explosive device. In this case the policeman said the terrorist had held a matchbox in the palm of his left hand and struck it upwards with the match attached to the fuse of the bomb which was in his right hand. The fuse and the match had left traces on his hands and that was proof enough. Also that the terrorist had refused to answer any questions, giving only his name and nothing else. To all other questions he would answer by whistling a tune.

Gokalp asked the policeman if prisoners were tortured, the sergeant laughed and asked him if he had heard tell of some forms of torture. Gokalp said he had heard of some cases where boiling eggs were placed under people's armpits to make them talk.

★ ★ ★ ★ ★

When he got back home he was told he must not go out again. He felt restrained and restless in the confines of the courtyard. Soon after his return at noon the curfew was lifted and life had returned to the street. He wanted to see that. He went out of the front door and walked up to the end of the alleyway looking up and down the street. His mother came running after him and rebukingly led him back.

This time he went to the far end of the garden. At a loss to what to do, he climbed the almond tree and sat on the branch which was his lookout post when playing cowboys and Indians as children with his friends. He was not happy with the restrictions on his movements and wondered when they would be lifted. They could not restrict him forever he thought.

He had no idea nor did anyone else that tomorrow he would be gone, never to return.

In the afternoon, when an inspector came to the house and told his mother to prepare a suitcase for Gokalp to take with him to Nicosia where he was to go, everyone was surprised. He more than everyone else. His father had been informed, the inspector had said, and would take delivery of his son in Nicosia Police Headquarters. The inspector told him again not to go out or talk to anyone about his leaving for Nicosia.

Keeping the news quiet was something difficult. His grandmother was sent for. On the way back after delivering the message his sister Tumer stopped and told anyone curious enough to ask what was happening. She had only been told not to tell it to anyone before she told it to her grandmother. By the time the grandmother arrived the news had reached in whispers every mother in the neighbourhood.

The cash resources of the family were pooled and his mother went out to shop for his impending journey. She came back with a new cardboard suitcase and pyjamas.

That evening he sat in the courtyard listening to his grandmother tell him not for the first time the morning of his birth. The morning of his coming into the world.

He listened to her with all his attention. A storm was raging outside, she told him. It had started to blow at the same time as his mother first felt the pangs. The midwife arrived wrapped in a cotton blanket to ward off the biting cold of the night. At first they had nothing to do but wait. They sat in the light of the flickering oil lamp around the charcoal fire and warmed themselves and listened to the storm gather in strength outside.

As the storm intensified outside his mother's pangs became frequent inside. Through the gap at the bottom of the door and crevices in the windows came the wind and cold to reach every nook in the first floor room of the one-up-two-down stone-built flat-roofed white washed house with an outside stairway and balcony made of wood. Through the same crevices came blue-white lightning flashes and thunder to strafe the room. The storm was overhead when his mother laboured in childbirth.

When he was born and the midwife held him upside down and slapped his backside, his first cry was lost to the cracking of lightning and the thunderbolt that fell on the minaret a hundred yards away.

The storm had died out soon after. His grandmother came out on the balcony, it was the dawn of the day, yet she saw the one bright star in the sky. The same one she now pointed out to him saying "That is your star, the brightest star in the sky".

His grandmother believed that when a child is born a new star shines in the sky and when a person died that person's star dims and goes out with him. When his grandmother finished telling him this, she took his face into her hands, she kissed him on both eyes and held him to her bossom. He was filled with emotion and love for her, when he looked up she had quiet tears in her eyes.

In the morning the police came in their Land Rovers, one to the front of his house, blocking the road and the entrance to the alleyway, the other to that of his father's cousin's house at the back separated by the tall garden wall. The sergeant then told him to climb over the wall at the back and go to the house of his father's cousins, where a Land Rover was waiting to take him to Nicosia.

He said his farewells to his mother and grandmother and to the neighbour, the stone mason's wife who came into the courtyard to wish him Godspeed. Then he took his cardboard case in his hand, and walked to the end of the garden. He waved at his young brother and the mason's children who called out cheerfully farewell after him and jumped over the garden wall to the waiting escort, to be driven away, never to return to the house again.

He asked the policemen escorting him if they would allow him to take his leave from his friends and teachers at school. It was too dangerous they said. Their orders were to take him non-stop to Police headquarters in Nicosia. He left Paphos without saying goodbye to any of his friends or teachers. Beyond the village of Yeroskipu a sense in him forbade him to venture further. He knew it was impossible to do. He looked back at the distant familiar sights and felt at a loss. But he soon came out of it when he started to think what lay ahead in Nicosia and the sense of adventure took hold of him.

He was given a pair of dark glasses and told to wear them so as not to be recognised. He found this comical, thinking that in all probability he would be taken for another terrorist on the way to serve his sentence. That is precisely what people on the way did think. In the streets of the villages which they passed through, he heard them shout this at him, "There goes another one". Be they Greek or Turk the words spoken by the people were the same words, "There goes another one", but to each it conveyed different meaning and stirred different emotion.

★★★★★

The Land Rover drove to the police station in Kyrenia Street in Nicosia where he was handed over to his father's care. Their immediate concern was to find a place for him to stay. His cousin had moved to Limasol by then so they had no relatives who could put him up. They eventually decided to ask help from the leader of the Turkish Community, Dr. Kutchuk, who was also a trustee of the Turkish Lycee and the boarding house for students.

They walked across the road from the police station to the newspaper office which Dr. Kutchuk ran. This operated on the ground floor and his living quarters were above. His father explained to a clerk his reason for a call

Gökalp's father at Athalasia training camp for police commondos, seated wearing the uniform. Picture taken 5th February 1956.

Dr. Fazıl Kutchuk (cantre) with Dr. İhsan Ali (right) and Derviş Ahmed Raşid.

YAŞA
DOĞACAKTIRSANA VADET
TİĞİ GÜNLER HAKKIN
KİMBİLİR BELKİ YARIN
BELKİ YARINDAN ŞİMDİ YAKIN

Dr. Fazıl Kutchuk carried on shoulders through the streets at Paphos.

on the leader of the community and asked if it was possible to see him now. Not to be autdone by the Cypriot Greek Youth, at Paphos, Gokalp and his friends had taken to the school yard to shout "Cyprus is Turkish and will remain Turkish", and "ya, ya, ya, sha, sha, sha, Doctor Kutchuk çok yasha" (long live Doctor Kutchuk) the day after Dr. Kutchuk's newspaper Halkın Sesi (People's Voice) carried the editorial view: "Cyprus is Turkish". And here he was at the lion's den to ask help from Dr. Kutchuk.

After a wait at the bottom of the wooden stairs, Dr. Kutchuk appeared at the top with a cigarette dangling from his mouth. He had at least three days growth of stubble on his face and his shirt was open down the front.

He took a couple of steps down and then stood there, asking what he could do for them.

His father then began to explain why they were there asking him for help. The Doctor's reaction was one of anger, and he declared that he could do nothing help them as it was no concern of his. His father then begged the leader to have the boy placed in school so as not to lose a year of his studies leading up to his final examinations. The doctor repeated in anger that it did not concern him in the least.

The doctor's attitude to them had puzzled Gokalp. He thought him very rude and supercilious in his manner. This he had not expected from a leader he had met for the very first time.

As his father started to beg again, the boy for the first time raised his voice and told his father to stop begging from this man who stood at the top of the stairs, and to leave immediately. He had suffered the humiliation of seeing his father beg for his son. His dignity was affronted and he showed it thus. With his cardboard suitcase in his hand, he turned and left, and his father trailed out after him.

At the door he glanced back. Dr. Kutchuk was still standing there, the cigarette stub stuck in the corner of his open mouth.

Out in the street he asked his father why was the doctor so rude and unhelpful? His father kept silent. Gokalp wondered if it had anything to do with his uncle by marriage, Dr Ihsan, his father's brother-in-law and Dr. Kutchuk? Their rivalry and animosity to each other went back to their days at university. He asked his father if it was because of this that they were refused help. His father chose to keep silent.

This time they made their way to Athalasia, the police commando training camp where his father was stationed. While he sat in a tent and watched police commandos train in the use of handguns, in a wooden mock up of a narrow street, his father went to see his commanding officer, Major Scott.

When his father returned he was with the Major. He saw them walk in the midday sun towards the tent, and as the Major entered all the non-commissioned officers there stood to attention. Major Scott spoke briefly to Gokalp and left.

His father then told him that Major Scott had got in touch with Field Marshall Sir John Harding, the Governor of Cyprus, and told the Field Marshal of the plight they were in, requesting his help.

The call came in the afternoon and Gokalp was taken back to Nicosia where he registered at the Turkish Lycee and, at the same time, a bed was found for him in the dormitory.

* * * * *

On his first evening in Nicosia, he was surprised to find that the boy in the next bunk to his in his dormitory was none other than Ozgun, a friend from Paphos. They had spent many childhood days playing together and watching the silkworms, kept on trays in a special room, chew on mulberry leaves. Later they would watch the silkworm weave a cocoon from which the silk was extracted. They had looked upon the work of the caterpillars in wonder and waited to see next year, not knowing how or why a metamorphosis took place, and the worm inside ate a hole in the cocoon to emerge as a butterfly and to couple and lay eggs which then became larvae and then caterpillars to weave the cocoon from which the silk was extracted.

He learned from Ozgun that two other boys from Paphos were also at the school, but shared a room at a house in one of the new suburbs outside the walls of the city. The house where the EOKA gunman called, looking for him.

And here he was on his last evening in Nicosia, safe in the residence of the Chief Justice of Cyprus.

His last waking thought that night, as he lay in bed, turned to the time beyond, to the future, to what lay ahead awaiting him. He was leaving the island. As long as the terrorism continued he knew he could not come back. But one day he hoped to return. And when that day came he would fly over Paphos, piloting his own plane to despite his father. The people would look up and see him return. Tomorrow he would fly to a new world to a new life that awaited him, alone. Earlier his teacher, Mr Rofe, had brought a parting gift for him saying Gokalp would need it in England. It was a tweed jacket. He had hardly worn it he had said. It fitted Gokalp perfectly. Tomorrow he would wear it for his hurriedly arranged journey to his uncle in Istanbul to await there the decision concerning his future safety.

Tomorrow he would start on a journey in life he knew not where it would take him. He pondered about it. He had not been prepared for this. He felt a sudden anxiety. The road in front of him looked more like a dark tunnel. The future lay beyond that. Here he thought he was at the entrance to the future that awaited him. He looked at the tunnel and saw no light at the end of it. He felt uncertain about stepping forward into this dark space. He had no other choice. He had to brave it. He was glad he was on his way. He was glad to have escaped alive and unhurt. Also glad to have had the opportunity which would take him to other lands and to new experiences. With this thought he stepped forward. His subconscious had taken over. He found himself in a dark void. He was dreaming in light sleep.

In the dark void he tried to move forward but felt unable to do so. An unknown and invisible force held him immobile. He felt his body paralysed yet his mind struggled and fought fiercely ordering him forward but to no avail. He felt fear. The fear of the unknown. A shiver ran through his body.

He woke up. His dream had frightened him. He was in bed warm and safe. There was no need to be frightened of, to struggle against an unknown force in a dream. Why shouldn't he surrender his will to the control of the unknown force in his subconscious world to journey to its limits as his life was now controlled in his conscious world by others? It is a dream after all. To dream....

He submitted his will to the force in his subconscious and could feel the energy which had held him tense and immobile drain from his body. He began to levitate. This was the most peaceful sensation he had ever experienced. He was no longer in a void but over

Paphos moving at will above the street where he had lived seeing people at their daily life and they in return looking up at him pointing him to each other. Then he found himself again in the dark void. But this time he was inside a radiant translucent silk cocoon woven around him by the force. Like a space capsule it stood ready to travel through silent darkness. He saw himself inside the cocoon willing for the voyage. Weightless and effortless he felt momentum and saw the white transparent cocoon with him inside distance itself and become a spectrum in a particle of light in the vast and eternal dark void.

And so he fell deeply asleep.

★ ★ ★ ★ ★

Addendum. The story you have just read is a true story. I am Gokalp.

It was my intention when I completed writing this story ten years ago, in March 1987, to cloak the characters in it under fictitious names, except of course the prominent politicians or personages of the day who have become part of the history of Cyprus.

Had I done that I think I would have committed an unforgivable act, and a loss to all time the lives of the people of Paphos. For, far from the politicians, the events in Cyprus affected the lives of ordinary people, men, women and children who have lived right through the times to the present, in all hundreds of thousands, with many a good story and dramatic events to tell than those lived by me.

I therefore decided, just before taking it to the printers, not only to give the true identity of those who are in the book but also to illustrate it with pictures which are available to me.

Thirty, or indeed, forty years on, although I share the same memories, the boy Gokalp had lived in a different world in form and essence than I am living now. His experience in life shaped the man in me. Yet a man of fifty seven, or indeed, a man of forty six, when I started to write the story, cannot be a boy of sixteen except in memory. Therefore I feel it is natural that I refer to him in third person singular.

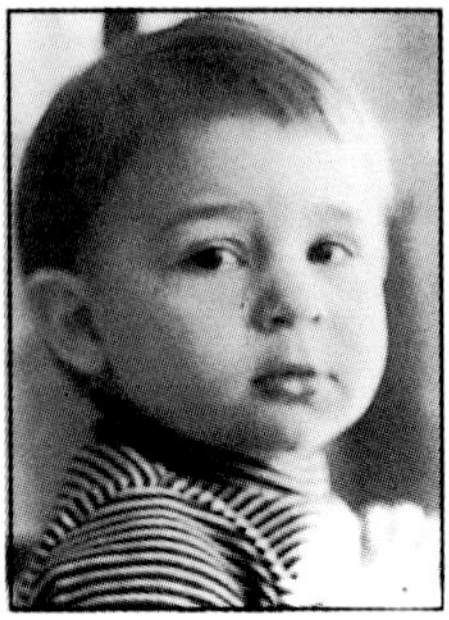

This book is a memorial to all those men and women who are in it, in which they become immortal.

A book is an ever present friend, a constant companion. This book is written in memory of my forefathers and dedicated to my son in whom I see my forefathers.